THE BELIEVERS GUIDE FOR LEAVING CHURCH AND BECOMING EKKLESIA

The Believers Guide for
Leaving CHURCH Becoming EKKLESIA

ISBN 978-0-9712916-0-7 (Paperback)

ISBN 978-0-9988952-2-2 (Kindle)

Library of Congress Control Number: 2017918050

The mission of KINGDOM WORD PUBLICATIONS is to produce and distribute quality materials that will strengthen believers, and assist in planting and developing ministry works structured after New Testament patterns. We pray that these materials will aid in equipping leaders and help to lay firm biblical foundations that exalt the Lord Jesus Christ as He builds His ekklesia and extends His Kingdom in the earth.

For more information, visit our website
www.TheEkklesiaCenter.org

PUBLISHED BY KINGDOM WORD PUBLICATIONS
ALBION, MICHIGAN 49224 Printed in the U.S.A.

TABLE OF CONTENTS

...upon this rock I will build my [ekklesia]; and the gates of [hades] shall not prevail against it. And I will give unto thee the keys of the kingdom of heaven: and whatsoever thou shalt bind on earth shall be bound in heaven: and whatsoever thou shalt loose on earth shall be loosed in heaven.

(Matthew 16:18-19)

THE BELIEVERS GUIDE FOR LEAVING CHURCH AND BECOMING EKKLESIA

...upon this rock I will build my [ekklesia], and the Gates of [Hades] will not prevail against it! (Matthew 16:18)

You, no doubt, are among those who seek to understand ekklesia. This book, THE BELIEVERS GUIDE FOR LEAVING CHURCH AND BECOMING EKKLESIA will help you do two things:

- First, it will provide you with a better understanding of ekklesia and its importance in your life.

- Second, it will help you navigate the steps you need to take in order to navigate the transition from 'church' into 'ekklesia'.

As the title indicates, this book is a guide. Ultimately, you must rely on the Holy Spirit to help you make this wonderful transition. The more you understand what the ekklesia is and its purpose in the earth, you can be among those who will turn families, neighborhoods, cities, states and beyond upside down with power from the Kingdom of Heaven.

WHAT DOES LEAVING CHURCH AND BECOMING EKKLESIA MEAN?

Leaving church is the intentional decision to leave religious systems that were instituted in the fourth century when Christianity became the state religion of Rome. Simultaneously; it is a return to the simple, organic gatherings prevalent in scripture.

The first Doctrine of Christ, that leads us to maturity is the foundation of repentance from dead works (Hebrews 6:1). The idea of 'leaving church' is to disconnect from dead and man-made religious practices that do nothing to empower, build, or release you into your destiny.

Becoming ekklesia implies a progressive change. It is becoming what Jesus declared He would build. When He led His disciples to the coast of Caesarea Philippi, He was on a clear mission. This trek to a forbidden and foreboding place would culminate in the revelation of who He was, and simultaneously be the announcement that His eternal purpose would soon be activated through a special group of believers – the ekklesia

WHO IS JESUS?

When Jesus came into the coasts of Caesarea Philippi, he asked his disciples, saying, "Whom do men say that I the Son of man am?" And they said, "Some say that thou art John the Baptist: some, Elias; and others, Jeremias, or one of the prophets" (Matthew 16:13-14)

For over two years the disciples had traveled with Jesus from city to city, and had witnessed His interaction among many people. Surely, they had heard people discuss who they assumed He was. The answer they gave clearly exposed the skewed religious mindset of many people. They saw Jesus as the reincarnation of one of the dead prophets.

Jesus was a living man, walking among them, healing the sick, feeding multitudes and raising the dead. So, what would be the disciples' response to this same query?

He saith unto them, "But whom say ye that I am?" And Simon Peter answered and said, "Thou art the Christ, the Son of the living God." (Matthew 16:15-16)

Scripture does not indicate if Peter answered immediately or if there was some awkward silence among the disciples at first. It is clear, however, that he gave the right answer. What he stated was not just a declaration of faith, it was the revelation that every believer must carry in their heart – that Jesus is the Christ, Son of the Living God. This is the only way you or I can enter and be effective in the ekklesia.

For a brief moment, the Holy Spirit opened Peter's eyes to see Jesus in a completely new dimension. Jesus made it clear that neither flesh and blood, or normal comprehension could produce that level of understanding. It required revelation prompted by God Himself (Matthew 16:17).

DEFINING REVELATION

Revelation is the process used by the Holy Spirit to unveil, uncover and clarify divine truth. It is both inclusive and exclusive.

REVELATION IS INCLUSIVE

Inclusive means that revelation is AVAILABLE to everyone. Availability, however, is not a guarantee that everyone will receive it. Like salvation, it is available to all; but not everybody will desire it.

Religious tradition can limit your ability to receive revelation. The reason the religious leaders of the first century struggled to understand Jesus, stemmed primarily from the fact that they did not have a revelation of who He was (Mark 6:3; John 6:42).

Today, many people only know Jesus as portrayed by their denominational traditions. As a result, their view is often limited to what Jesus does, rather than who He is (John 2:23-25).

REVELATION IS EXCLUSIVE

Revelation is also exclusive. It is designed by God to only be seen by those who qualify to see it.

> And he said unto them, "Unto you it is given to know the mystery of the kingdom of God: but unto them that are without, all these things are done in parables: That seeing they may see, and not perceive; and hearing they may hear, and not understand; lest at any time they should be converted, and their sins should be forgiven them. "(Mark 4:11-12)

Some truths that are revealed to you are hidden from others. This explains why two people can see the same thing, and have completely different conclusions. With Jesus Christ, it is critical that we all have the same revelation - that Jesus is the Christ, Son of the Living God. That is the only way to understand the ekklesia.

How to Walk in Revelation?

There is no formula that produces revelation. The Holy Spirit reveals to us what we need to know.

> But as it is written, Eye hath not seen, nor ear heard, neither have entered into the heart of man, the things which God hath prepared for them that love him. But God hath revealed them unto us by his Spirit: for the Spirit searcheth all things, yea, the deep things of God. (1Corinthians 2:9-10)

> Wherefore I give you to understand, that no man speaking by the Spirit of God calleth Jesus accursed: and that no man can say that Jesus is the Lord, but by the Holy Ghost. (1Corinthians 12:3)

Revelation never contradicts the written Word of God. It is divine information that can give us a clear understanding of any situation we encounter.

Revelation begins when you confess that Jesus is Lord. When you first surrendered to Jesus Christ, it was necessary that you declare Him as your Lord (Romans 10:9-10). This should not be a one-time confession. You should declare it all the time. In every situation and circumstance, you must declare that Jesus is Lord. When you do, you are acknowledging that He owns everything, and that He has authority in all matters concerning your life (Galatians 2:20).

In tough times, you may not 'feel' like He is Lord, but declare it anyway. You want the Holy Spirit to know you are fully submitted to the will of the Lord (1 Corinthians 1:3).

I confess His Lordship nearly every day. It is important to me to declare that, 'God is still on the throne, the devil is defeated, and Jesus is Lord!' The musicians who serve us have written a song with these words as the key lyrics. We close our public gatherings by saying this together. It is a constant reminder to us of the Lordship of Jesus Christ.

In addition to this, I believe that all doctrine stems from five basic values in the New Testament. There are times when the values are obscured, and it requires apostolic doctrines to bring them back into clarity.

The first and most primary value we embrace is the Lordship of Jesus Christ over our lives. Submitting to Him as Lord precedes everything we believe or do. Declaring Him as Lord is encased in the knowledge that He is alive (Hebrews 7:25; Revelation 1:18). If we overlook, miss or ignore this value, then all other values are worthless.

Jesus will not build His ekklesia with anyone who does not have the revelation that He is the Christ, Son of the Living God. Start confessing His Lordship over your life now. More and more, the Holy Spirit will reveal Jesus Christ to you beyond what you have ever known (John 15:26).

PETER'S TWO-PART REVELATION

The revelation Peter received had two parts. First, there was the declaration that Jesus is the Christ, the anointed. He was not merely 'a Christ', but rather 'the' Christ.

Jesus had led the disciples to the occult ridden place called Caesarea Philippi. It was where Pan, a god of perversion was worshipped. It was where a literal place called the Gate of Hades existed. Both human and animal sacrifices regularly took place at this demonic location.

At Caesarea Philippi you could see the likenesses of dead Caesars carved into the mountain. These dead Caesars were deified by their followers and to be considered 'Christs'. Remember, Jesus warned his followers that there would be many declaring that they were Christ (Matthew 24:5).

Peter's revelation set Jesus apart from all other self-proclaimed Christs. God had anointed Jesus with power, through which He performed many miracles (Acts 10:38). He was 'the Christ' – not merely 'a Christ!'

Second, Peter declared that Jesus was the Son of the Living God. Undoubtedly, most Jews believed God to be living, but now before them was a man who was purported to be His Living Son. Let that sink in for a moment. The human being the Jews saw standing before them was claiming that the Living God was His Father (Matthew 16:17; John 5:18; 10:30)

Ancient writings declared God as the father of Abraham, Isaac and Jacob. He had led Isaiah, Jeremiah, all the old testament prophets and, even, John the Baptist. At the time Jesus and His disciples were at Caesarea Philippi, these people were all dead.

The Jews had been waiting for a Messiah, and now Peter's revelation could, potentially, bring an end to their wait. He declared Jesus as the Living Son of the Living God.

Before I go any further, you must understand that this truth has not changed. He is still the Living Son of the Living God. Even though Jesus lived and walked the earth two-thousand years ago; and even though He was crucified and buried in a borrowed tomb; the Word of God declares that He rose from the dead and was seen by hundreds of people after His resurrection (1Corinthians 15:1-6). Scripture declares that He lives, and is seated at the right hand of the Father interceding for you and me (Mark 16:19; Romans 8:34; Hebrews 1:3; 1Peter 3:22).

This is important. You and I must have the same revelation Peter had. We must know without a shadow of a doubt, that Jesus is truly the Christ and that He is the LIVING Son of the LIVING God. Jesus is still alive!

Then charged he his disciples that they should tell no man that he was Jesus the Christ. (Matthew 16:20 KJV)

Why would Jesus charge His disciples not to tell anyone that He was Jesus the Christ? It is because He is building His ekklesia with those who have the revelation – not just information, of who He is. People with 'information' are limited to what they are told. They are apt to second guess themselves in times of crisis.

A person with the revelation of Jesus as the Christ, Son of the Living God, will have an inward 'knowing' that Jesus is alive and will act accordingly. Revelation does not require the need to physically see Him. It is an inward knowing that He is there to confirm His Word in you with signs and wonders (Mark 16:19-20).

Those with a revelation of Jesus Christ will walk in confidence. They boldly cast out devils, heal the sick and perform many signs and wonders in the authority of the risen and living Lord.

Start confessing throughout each day, that Jesus is the Christ, Son of the Living God. In every matter, situation or circumstance, make this declaration. Your Living Lord, Son of the Living God will be with you to empower you (Matthew 28:20). The Holy Spirit will guide you every step of the way (John 16:13). And, He will validate that you are also an empowered son of God (Romans 8:14-16; Galatians 4:6).

EKKLESIA AND GOD'S ORIGINAL INTENT

What does the Kingdom Mandate (Genesis 1:28), have to do with what took place at Caesarea Philippi? Will God's original intent for man be restored?

> And God said, **Let us make man in our image, after our likeness: and let them have dominion** over the fish of the sea, and over the fowl of the air, and over the cattle, and over all the earth, and over every creeping thing that creepeth upon the earth. So **God created man in his own image, in the image of God created he him**; male and female created he them. And God blessed them, and God said unto them, **Be fruitful, and multiply, and replenish the earth, and subdue it: and have dominion** over the fish of the sea, and over the fowl of the air, and over every living thing that moveth upon the earth (Genesis 1:26-28)

When God created man, He clearly declared mankind's identity, capacity, and authority.

Man's identity was found in that God created him in His image. Man's capacity was revealed when God declared that man would have dominion. And finally, man's authority was given when God commanded him to subdue the earth.

When man disobeyed God, his identity became distorted. Instead of walking in the image of God, he became self-aware of his inadequacies (Genesis 3:10). Sin limited man's capacity. He could no longer consume freely from the Garden, but had to force the ground to produce from the sweat of his brow (Genesis 3:17-19). Man's authority shifted from managing the earth to controlling, conquering and enslaving each other (Genesis 3:16).

God immediately set in motion a plan in the earth for man to fulfill His original mandate to be fruitful, to multiply, replenish and subdue the earth. Through seven covenants, God meticulously restored the relationship He had with His greatest creation – man. This is why the event at Caesarea Philippi is so important to us. Both the relationship God desired to have with man, and the purpose for placing man in the earth was revealed by Jesus Christ.

A New Day Is Dawning

The combination of man realizing who Jesus is and Jesus conferring the keys of the Kingdom of Heaven to man, along with the restored authority to bind and loose on earth whatever has been bound or loosed in heaven, showed that a new day was dawning. Once again, mankind's identity, capacity and authority were being revealed.

First, only a specific group will be entrusted to carry the Lord's mandate forward. We discover their identity from what they know. They would be identified as those who have the revelation that Jesus is the Christ, Son of the Living God.

Second, their capacity was established when Jesus declared that the Gates of Hades would not be able to prevail against them. And third, the authority of this called out group would be activated when Jesus gave them the keys of the Kingdom of Heaven. They would have the authority to legislate the policies of Heaven in the earth.

Who is this specific group of people? It is the ekklesia. The called-out assembly of believers Jesus declared He would build. It is the ekklesia consisting of believers like you that will fulfill the original mandate to be fruitful, to multiply, to replenish and subdue the earth.

Soon after this moment at Caesarea Philippi, Jesus would purchase the ekklesia with His blood (Acts 20:28). The apostle Paul declared that through it, the wisdom of God would be made known to principalities and powers. (Ephesian 3:10). They would become known as the assembly of the Living God, the very pillar and ground of truth (1Timothy 3:15).

What does this mean to you? It means that you can be empowered by the Lord Jesus Christ to impact the earth. Everything intended by God in creation is now available to you.

EKKLESIA EXPLAINED

The Greek word 'ekklesia' (pronounced eh-clay-see-ah), is found 115 times in the New Testament. It is a combination of two Greek words; *ek* which means to be 'out of' or 'away from', and *kaleo* which is translated 'to call'. Together, as ekklesia, ek and kaleo generally mean 'to call out'.

If that was all to the word 'ekklesia'; then there would be little to concern ourselves with in this matter. But there is much more hidden that you will soon discover. There is more to ekklesia than just a group of people who would be called out. The question must be asked, "What were they called out for?"

The answer to this question requires an understanding of the ekklesia in its historical context.

The concept of a group being called out could be traced back into the Old Testament. The word *qahal*, is the Old Testament equivalent of ekklesia. In the Septuagint, the Hebrew word *qahal* is translated into Greek as ekklesia. The basic words often associated with ekklesia in the Old Testament are; multitude (Genesis 48:4); assembly (Exodus 12:6; Acts 19:32); and congregation (Leviticus 4:14). (A full study of *qahal* is recommended).

The Old Testament references give a hint as to why Jesus said He would build an ekklesia. It is an interesting choice. He had other options. He could have said that He would build His *hieron*, which the Greek word translated as temple. After all, the temple was the most sacred place for Jews. He could have also opted to build His *sunagoge*. This would be the synagogue where most of the religious dialogue and teaching took place.

The model Jesus chose was the ekklesia, which in the eyes of most people in His day was no longer a sacred gathering of Jews, but rather a secular governmental entity. Unlike the temple or synagogue, ekklesia had lost its religious association.

I trust you are beginning to see that simply being called out is not the whole picture. The historical reason as to WHY they were called is of greater importance. It was a group of citizens that were called out to conduct business for the government.

The Roman government was in power during the lifetime of Jesus. The concept of the ekklesia had been around for hundreds of years. In Jesus' day, it had become known as an arm of the government. The Romans had borrowed the concept from the Greeks and used it to establish the policies of Rome throughout its empire. Everyone knew that the ekklesia had authority to act on behalf of the governor of a territory.

This is important to understand. This secular model Jesus used had authority. It had the full backing of Rome. The Roman ekklesia could confer or deny citizenship, elect officials, establish policies, and generally legislate the policies of Rome in the territory they served.

What does this mean to us? Just like the Roman ekklesia represented its government, the ekklesia Jesus would build would represent Him and His government – the Kingdom of Heaven.

STOP.

DO **EXERCISE A: What Are We Doing?** BEFORE READING THE NEXT SECTION (Page 49)

THE EKKLESIA – THEN AND NOW

If you completed Exercise A, you should have a list of three or more things you are doing to represent the Kingdom of Heaven in the earth. There were no right or wrong answers, it is a good beginning point for you.

In this section we will examine the authority of Jesus' ekklesia. The Word of God will give you an opportunity to realize what you may have missed in your previous list.

Scripture records Jesus only speaking of ekklesia twice. It is blaringly obvious that He did not spend time explaining what it was. The reason is that the disciples clearly understood what the ekklesia was, and more importantly, what it did.

In these two brief references, Jesus gives us a treasure trove of information that can unlock our understanding of the modern day ekklesia.

> And I say also unto thee, That thou art Peter, and upon this rock I will build my [ekklesia]; and the gates of [hades] shall not prevail against it. And I will give unto thee the keys of the kingdom of heaven: and whatsoever thou shalt bind on earth shall be bound in heaven: and whatsoever thou shalt loose on earth shall be loosed in heaven. (Matthew 16:18-19 KJV)

> Moreover if thy brother shall trespass against thee, go and tell him his fault between thee and him alone: if he shall hear thee, thou hast gained thy brother. But if he will not hear thee, then take with thee one or two more, that in the mouth of two or three witnesses every word may be established. And if he shall neglect to hear them, tell it unto the [ekklesia]: but if he neglect to hear the [ekklesia], let him be unto thee as an heathen man and a publican. Verily I say unto you, Whatsoever ye shall bind on earth shall be bound in heaven: and whatsoever ye shall loose on earth shall be loosed in heaven. Again I say unto you, That if two of you shall agree on earth as touching any thing that they shall ask, it shall be done for them of my Father which is in heaven. For where two or three are gathered together in my name, there am I in the midst of them. (Matthew 18:15-20 KJV)

First, Jesus declared the qualifications for access into ekklesia. It is the revelation that He is the Christ, Son of the Living God. We have already discussed the importance of having this revelation, and will repeat this over and over again throughout this guide. Along with this revelation, Jesus declares the building process, the capacity, the tools and the authority of the ekklesia.

20

THE BUILDING PROCESS OF THE EKKLESIA

Upon this rock I will build my ekklesia…(Matthew 16:18). Jesus first makes it clear that He will build an ekklesia that belonged to Him.

In my book, NO LONGER CHURCH AS USUAL Second Edition, I shared a concept that will help you understand the Lord's process of building His ekklesia. At the time I wrote that book I still thought church and ekklesia were the same. Therefore, I am adjusting the concept to reflect the accurate understanding of ekklesia. Here is the concept:

THE EKKLESIA IS A HUMAN STRUCTURE, BUILT BY DIVINE PATTERN, FOR ETERNAL PURPOSES.

Jesus is building the ekklesia in the earth. The earth is where the ekklesia functions. It is designed to implement Kingdom policies and purposes in the earth. You and I, who have the revelation of Jesus as the Christ, Son of the Living God are the building materials He needs to build the ekklesia. Notice the following passages:

For every house is builded by some man; but he that built all things is God. And Moses verily was faithful in all his house, as a servant, for a testimony of those things which were to be spoken after; But Christ as a son over his own house; whose house are we, if we hold fast the confidence and the rejoicing of the hope firm unto the end. (Hebrews 3:4-6)

And are built upon the foundation of the apostles and prophets, Jesus Christ himself being the chief corner stone; In whom all the building fitly framed together groweth unto an holy temple in the Lord: In whom ye also are builded together for an habitation of God through the Spirit. (Ephesians 2:20-22)

Ye also, as lively stones, are built up a spiritual house, an holy priesthood, to offer up spiritual sacrifices, acceptable to God by Jesus Christ. (1Peter 2:5)

Buildings are designed to function in the earth. That is why the ekklesia is first a human structure. It is made up of earthly materials known to humans. The ekklesia is not an angelic structure. The ekklesia follows the pattern of the Ark of the Covenant (Exodus 25:10-21), The Tabernacle (Exodus 26), and Noah's Ark (Genesis 6:14-16) which were all constructed using material known to men on the earth.

Revelation is the bonding agent that connects all components of the ekklesia together. It is the common bond that holds the five-fold ministers, the elders, the deacons, and any other function in the building or body in its proper place. This is what Jesus is building.

THE CAPACITY OF THE EKKLESIA

Jesus knew that the ekklesia would need to be empowered to function in a world where the enemy would attack it from many dimensions. If it were ill equipped, it would be easily defeated.

After announcing that He would build His ekklesia, Jesus declared that "... the gates of hades shall not prevail against it. (Matthew 16:18)." He made it abundantly clear that what He was building could not be defeated. This would be true under all circumstances. Hades gates would not prevail. This spoke directly to the capacity of the ekklesia.

To understand this, we need to look at the definition of the word capacity. The Merriman-Webster dictionary reveals five distinct characterizations of the word capacity, four of which has direct implications to the Lord's ekklesia.

- **LEGAL COMPETENCY** The ekklesia must be fully versed in the policies of the Kingdom. Throughout His ministry, Jesus taught the disciples the in's and out's of the Kingdom. He taught and demonstrated the influence, the power and the purpose of the Kingdom in the lives of believers. The ekklesia must realize that it functions from a Kingdom perspective. The importance of this will be shown later in this booklet.

- **THE POTENTIAL OR SUITABILITY FOR HOLDING, STORING OR ACCOMMODATING** The ekklesia must position itself to receive anyone who has the revelation that Jesus is the Christ, Son of the Living God. Capacity could refer to the total number that can be contained. However, in the ekklesia it can organically hold as many as the Lord shall save (Acts 2:47).

- **AN INDIVIDUAL'S MENTAL OR PHYSICAL ABILITY** The ability to overcome world systems through the ekklesia is not based on human strength. Often we read where the apostles

23

were overcome physically by their enemies (Acts 5:40; 8:1; 16:23), but their victory was in the fact that they had been with Jesus (Luke 21:15; Acts 4:13; 6:8-10; 2Corinthians 12:9).

- **THE FACILITY OR POWER TO PRODUCE, PERFORM, OR DEPLOY** The ekklesia is organic. Thus, it has the innate ability to grow in the most adverse environments. Within that growth is the expansion of the Kingdom of God in the earth. The original mandate given to man in the garden reveals its dynamic ability. The command to be fruitful, to multiply and replenish, to subdue the earth and to have dominion can be realized today as believers walk in obedience. Jesus' marching orders to 'go into all the world and make disciples of nations' is built into the DNA of the ekklesia.

Consider the state of the contemporary 'church system'. It is divided by doctrinal, ideological and racial lines. It is so infused with compromise and acquiescing to the worlds systems that it is virtually useless in real warfare against sin. Often, what is clearly an abomination against God, is accommodated and renamed as 'human nature'. The influence of Hades runs rampant throughout the 'church world'.

The ekklesia should reflect Jesus in the earth. Instead, as the 'church', it became an identity totally foreign to what Jesus intended. As such, it exhibits nothing near the capacity Jesus decreed upon the ekklesia.

... Thus saith the LORD of hosts; Turn ye unto me, saith the LORD of hosts, and I will turn unto you, saith the LORD of hosts. (Zechariah 1:3)

Israel had strayed from the Lord – sometimes willfully, and at other times ignorantly. Regardless, the impact on the nation was the same. They were overrun and subject to their enemies.

The switch from ekklesia to church was made over five hundred years ago. This has been unknown to most believers. Yet, the impact is still the same. The church is weak and ineffective expanding the Kingdom of Heaven into the earth.

The Holy Spirit is bringing the true identity of God's people to the forefront. When truth becomes known, response is mandated. A person will either accept or reject it. The same plea made to Israel is being made today. The Lord is saying, "Return to Me, and I will return to you." Once you realize that Jesus never said He would build a 'church', it becomes your decision to respond accordingly. As more believers submit to what Jesus intended, the capacity of the Body of Christ will take on new dimensions.

THE TOOLS OF THE EKKLESIA

The primary tool Jesus gave the ekklesia was the keys of the Kingdom of Heaven. Keys have a unique function. They provide a way to gain access into a secure area. A building or room that is locked can be easily accessed by anyone who has the appropriate key. Access any other way would be illegal. To be given the key to any area suggests that you can be trusted with everything in the area you've been given access to.

I use a bible software program that came with 23 bible translations, 26 commentaries, multiple dictionaries and lexicons with Greek and Hebrew translations of nearly every word in scripture. Yet, there were some bible translations that had to be purchased separately from the main program. To access these bibles, I was sent a code which was the *digital key* necessary to unlock a translation. Once I entered the digital key into the program, I gained full use of the additional bible translation.

This process reveals a powerful truth. The digital key I purchased gave me access to a bible translation that was ALREADY in the software program. The developer of the bible program did not send me any additional software. They provided me with a digital key to unlock a bible translation that was ALREADY imbedded in the program. The digital key gave me access to it. Likewise, everything the ekklesia needs, is ALREADY in the Kingdom of Heaven. The keys Jesus gave, simply provided access to all the Kingdom has available.

When Jesus declared He would build His ekklesia, He immediately promised the keys necessary to access His Kingdom. This is an important biblical pattern. Whenever God gives an assignment, He has also prepared all the resources needed to accomplish His will. Let's look at some examples.

And God blessed them, and God said unto them, Be fruitful, and multiply, and replenish the earth, and subdue it: and have dominion over the fish of the sea, and over the fowl of the air, and over every living thing that moveth upon the earth. And God said, **Behold, I have given you** every herb bearing seed, which is upon the face of all the earth, and every tree, in the which is the fruit of a tree yielding seed; to you it shall be for meat. (Genesis 1:28-29)

The mandate man was given in the Garden was powerful. From the very beginning, God equipped His creation with the tools to accomplish His will for them. "Behold, I have given you..." shows us that along with the assignment came divine provision. Man was given every herb bearing seed, and every tree and its fruit for food.

MOSES ASSIGNMENT TO BUILD THE TABERNACLE

Who serve unto the example and shadow of heavenly things, as Moses was admonished of God when he was about to make the tabernacle: for, See, saith he, that thou make all things according to the pattern shewed to thee in the mount. (Hebrews 8:5 KJV)

And the LORD spake unto Moses, saying, **See, I have called by name Bezaleel the son of Uri, the son of Hur**, of the tribe of Judah: And **I have filled him with the spirit of God, in wisdom, and in understanding, and in knowledge, and in all manner of workmanship**, (Exodus 31:1-3 KJV)

Then wrought Bezaleel and Aholiab, and every wise hearted man, in whom **the LORD put wisdom and understanding to know how to work all manner of work for the service of the sanctuary**, according to all that the LORD had commanded. (Exodus 36:1 KJV)

God instructed Moses to build the Tabernacle. He was very specific as to how it was to be constructed. This included both material and design. Along with His instructions to Moses, was the provision necessary to complete the task. "See, I have called by name Bazaleel...". God provided Moses with a man who had wisdom, understanding and knowledge in all manner of workmanship. Moses assignment was accompanied by divine provision.

SOLOMON'S ASSIGNMENT TO BUILD THE TEMPLE

And of all my sons, (for the LORD hath given me many sons,) he hath chosen Solomon my son to sit upon the throne of the kingdom of the LORD over Israel. And he said unto me, Solomon thy son, he shall build my house and my courts: for I have chosen him to be my son, and I will be his father. (1 Chronicles 28:5-6 KJV)

Then Huram the king of Tyre answered in writing, which he sent to Solomon, Because the LORD hath loved his people, he hath made thee king over them. Huram said moreover, Blessed be the LORD God of Israel, that made heaven and earth, who hath given to David the king a wise son, endued with prudence and understanding, that might build an house for the LORD, and an house for his kingdom. **And now I have sent a cunning man, endued with understanding**, of Huram my father's, The son of a woman of the daughters of Dan, and his father was a man of Tyre, **skilful to work in gold, and in silver, in brass, in iron, in stone, and in timber, in purple, in blue, and in fine linen, and in crimson; also to grave any manner of graving, and to find out every device which shall be put to him**, with thy cunning men, and with the cunning men of my lord David thy father. (2 Chronicles 2:11-14 KJV)

Solomon was about to embark on a twenty-year project to build the Temple of the Lord (1Kings 9:10). His father, David, had provided the financial resources he needed for the task. But it was out of David's relationship with Huram, the king of Tyre, that Solomon was provided a skilled architect, Hiram. This again shows how God provides what we need to fulfill His assignment.

YOUR ASSIGNMENT IN THE EARTH

What has God called you to do? Unfortunately, too many believers are unable to answer this question with any clarity. The 'church' system has limited divine assignments to duties performed in the local church. The pinnacle is to be called into ministry, which is often limited into pulpit preaching.

In this season of transition, God is calling people to be world changers. They are being called to confront the Gates of Hades. They are being called to impact business, government, media, education, entertainment, religion, and family. These assignments cannot be comfortably contained within the hierarchal structure of many church systems.

> According **as his divine power hath given unto us all things that pertain unto life and godliness**, through the knowledge of him that hath called us to glory and virtue: (2 Peter 1:3)

> What shall we then say to these things? If God be for us, who can be against us? He that spared not his own Son, but delivered him up for

us all, **how shall he not with him also freely give us all things?** (Romans 8:31-32)

Your assignment is always greater than your current understanding and capacity. God at times will send you on an assignment without giving you all the details. Most times you will find that you have insufficient resources to accomplish what God has called you to do. Yet, like the pattern clearly seen in scripture, God will provide you with whatever is necessary to fulfill His purpose.

THE AUTHORITY OF THE EKKLESIA

First, Jesus revealed that He would build His ekklesia. Second, He declared its capacity to be impenetrable by the gates of Hades. Third, He provided the tools within the Kingdom of Heaven, and finally, He declared the authority the ekklesia would have in the earth.

> And I say also unto thee, That thou art Peter, and upon this rock I will build my [ekklesia]; and the gates of [Hades] shall not prevail against it. And I will give unto thee the keys of the kingdom of heaven: and whatsoever thou shalt bind on earth shall be bound in heaven: and whatsoever thou shalt loose on earth shall be loosed in heaven. (Matthew 16:18-19 KJV)

> And if he shall neglect to hear them, tell it unto the [ekklesia]: but if he neglect to hear the [ekklesia], let him be unto thee as an heathen man and a publican. Verily I say unto you, Whatsoever ye shall bind on earth shall be bound in heaven: and whatsoever ye shall loose on earth shall be loosed in heaven. (Matthew 18:17-18 KJV)

There are only two instances where Jesus referenced the ekklesia, and both times He spoke of its authority to bind and loose.

Remember that the ekklesia in Jesus day represented the full authority of the Roman government. This earthy version of the ekklesia had the full authority to carry out the policies of the Roman government. The divine ekklesia that Jesus said He would build would represent the Kingdom of Heaven. This divine version would have the full authority to carry out the policies of the Kingdom of Heaven.

The terms, binding and loosing have extensive biblical connotations, far too many to cover in this booklet. However, we will hone in on the specific context that Jesus used these words in relationship to the ekklesia.

THE DICTIONARY OF BIBLICAL IMAGERY ©1998 by InterVarsity Christian Fellowship/USA, reveals that one aspect of binding and loosing is 'the efficacy of earthly decisions in spiritual matters in the heavenly realm' (page 92). It further explains that God gave authority to the apostles '…condone or prohibit, practices that might be sinful' (page 517).

NELSON'S ILLUSTRATED BIBLE DICTIONARY ©1986 Thomas Nelson Publishers, helps us to understand that the tense of the verbs used in both Matthew 16:18 and Matthew 18:18 indicate that whatever was bound or loosed was already established in the will of the Father (page 183). This all points to the authority entrusted to the ekklesia.

In our discovery of the capacity of the ekklesia, its legal competency was first on the list. If those serving in the ekklesia do not know the will of the Father, they will have no ability to effectively bind and loose.

After conferring the keys of the Kingdom of Heaven, Jesus said the ekklesia would be able to bind, prohibit and declare unlawful anything that was already prohibited or declared unlawful in heaven. Likewise, the ekklesia would be able to loose, release into the earth, and declare lawful and permissible anything that was declared as such in heaven. The ekklesia can fully represent the authority of the Kingdom of Heaven in the earth.

One area delegated to the earthly Roman ekklesia was the authority to confer or deny citizenship. The second time Jesus mentioned ekklesia was in context of citizenship. He outlined a clear process for dealing with conflicts between kingdom citizens. If unresolved at the interpersonal level, the matter would be dealt with by the ekklesia.

If the offending person refused the decision of the ekklesia, they would be considered in the same category of unrepentant sinners. Jesus concluded by reminding those listening that the ekklesia could declare what was lawful or unlawful (based in the policies of the Kingdom of Heaven).

The ekklesia still has that authority today. The policies of the Kingdom of Heaven must be enacted in the earth. Our prayer should always be, "Thy kingdom come, thy will be done in earth, as it is in heaven" (Matthew 6:10). As we seek the Lord, He will give strategies and divine tools to accomplish His will in the earth!

What are the Gates of Hades?

When Jesus led His disciples to the coast of Caesarea Philippi, He knew they would have a graphic picture of all He was about to teach them. Caesarea Philippi was a forbidden place for respectable Jews.

> ...and the gates of [Hades] shall not prevail against it (Matthew 16:18)

The word 'hell' in this passage is translated from the Greek word *Hades*. This is another important piece to understanding ekklesia. The reason is that Hades was as much a place as it is a philosophy.

Upon arrival to Caesarea Philippi, the disciples saw three significant things. There were the monuments to the Caesars who had died, the temple of the pagan god Pan, and a cave with a seemingly bottomless pool known as the Gate of

Hades. At this place both human and animal sacrifices took place.

Hades was also known among the trilogy of mythological gods. They were Zeus, the god of the skies, Poseidon, the god of the seas, and Hades, the god of the underworld. Everything about Hades, in practice and philosophy points to its occult nature. But what were the 'gates' of Hades? Gates are generally points of entry. These can be both natural and spiritual.

In his book, RETURN OF THE FIRST CHURCH ©2007, John Fenn wrote that, *"In Jesus' time, as in Old Testament times, the gates of a city represented the place of power and authority"*. He further wrote, *"The gates of a city are where the business of that city (or kingdom) takes place"*. (page 92). The gates are where the ruling authorities gather to make policies, plans and decisions.

It is at the gate of Hades that demonic policies, plans and decisions are formulated. It is at the gate of Hades where the underworld of darkness seeks to distort truth, but open from time to time to release demonic influence into the earth.

Gates are the separation point between two groups – one group on the inside, the other on the outside. When the gates are opened, purposely or forcefully, then both groups are exposed to each other. Jesus declared that these gates will not prevail against the ekklesia. No demonic authority can overcome what Jesus is building.

The ekklesia today is being reignited to confront the gates of Hades. Anywhere the dark philosophies of sin run rampant is being challenged. The realms of business, education, media, entertainment, government, religion and family must be purged of any demonic influence. The ekklesia has been given the keys to do this, and the gates of Hades will not prevail.

8 COMMON QUESTIONS AND ANSWERS ABOUT EKKLESIA

1. WHERE IS THE WORD 'EKKLESIA' FOUND IN THE BIBLE?

When Jesus declared what He would build, He clearly said that He would build His ekklesia. In most bibles, it has been translated as church.

The English word 'church' is an incorrect translation of the Greek word 'ekklesia'. It is found 115 times in the original language of the New Testament.

In three instances, ekklesia is accurately translated as assembly – *Acts 19:32, 39, 41*. For the translators to have used the word 'church', in these instances, it would have had negative implications to their agenda. It would have suggested the possibility of an unlawful or unruly gathering of the 'church'.

In addition to the times ekklesia is used in the New Testament, the Septuagint (the Greek translation of the Old Testament) translated the Hebrew word *qahal* as ekklesia. This reveals that ekklesia was a common concept prior to the time of Jesus Christ.

2. WHAT DOES THE WORD 'EKKLESIA' MEAN?

The word 'ekklesia' is a composite of two Greek words. *'Ek'* which means *'out from'*, and *'kaleo'* which means *'to call'*. Together, they refer to a group of people who are 'called out'. Ekklesia could be translated as 'assembly' or 'congregation', but not as 'church'.

Beyond the basic definition of the word 'ekklesia', is the historical meaning it had. As stated before, the concept of ekklesia existed throughout the Old Testament where it primarily was associated with the Hebrews who were called out to assemble before the Lord (Exodus 12:6).

Over time, the ekklesia became known as a group called out to conduct official business. The concept was borrowed by the Romans from the Greeks. The Romans used their version of the ekklesia to establish policies for its government.

The Roman ekklesia was empowered to defer or deny citizenship, elect officials, and establish policies. Their primary responsibility was to ensure that the policies of the Roman governor was enforced in a territory. It is this model of ekklesia that was commonly known by people living during the time of Christ.

3. WHY IS IT IMPORTANT TO UNDERSTAND WHAT EKKLESIA MEANS?

Ekklesia expresses the identity, authority and purpose of the Body of Christ. Because of the mistranslation, Christians have embraced an identity completely different from the Lord's intent. Because the identity is wrong, their authority has often been misguided and their purpose has been buried in religious sectarianism.

The change from ekklesia to church, literally changed the trajectory of the Body of Christ. Instead of being a powerful ruling council under the Headship of Jesus Christ; it became an institution controlled by man. The church is more concerned with survival than it is with soul winning.

It is important to understand ekklesia to know who Christ intends you to be.

4. WHAT'S WRONG WITH THE WORD 'CHURCH'?

Many good people are active in the current church system; but it is not what Jesus intended for them. The English word 'church' is translated from the Greek word *kuriakon*. It generally means, 'of the lord'. That would appear to be acceptable until you learn the facts behind why the word 'church' was inserted to replace ekklesia.

Generally, when people hear the word 'church', they think of the building they go to; the denomination they belong to, and the doctrines they embrace. These images are incorrect.

Like the word 'ekklesia', the word 'church' expresses an identity. Its identity reveals the level of authority and general purpose. But it must be clearly understood that any concept of 'church' is not what Jesus said, or intended for His followers.

The facts regarding the word 'church' has been available for hundreds of years, the Holy Spirit is highlighting it in this season. Understanding your correct identity as the ekklesia is critical. Jesus is still building His ekklesia. His ekklesia will impact every sphere of human existence.

5. HOW DID THE GREEK WORD 'EKKLESIA' GET MISTRANSLATED AS CHURCH?

First, remember that ekklesia is NOT the Greek word for Church. The English word 'church' is a mistranslation. It is important that you understand that this mistranslation was done on purpose – it was not an accident.

This is the most important thing for you to understand. The very fact that ekklesia was willfully mistranslated by the instructions of an ungodly monarch, should alert you to the importance of the correct translation. Why would satan use this self-serving king to hide the truth of ekklesia from you?

King James may have ordered the mistranslation to protect his hierarchal authority, but satan has used it to weaken God's people. Millions of unsuspecting believers have accepted an identity never intended or assigned to them.

Here is a summary of how ekklesia was mistranslated as church:

- King James was opposed to anyone questioning the authority or decisions of a king. He believed kings were gods.
- He appointed himself as the head of the Church of England, through which he ruled it with bishops he selected
- In 1611, He convened a team of 52 scholars to produce a translation of the bible that would bear his name
- He gave them a list of 15 instructions they were to follow in the process of translating the biblical text. It was the 3rd instruction that specifically told them to mistranslate the word 'ekklesia' as church.

The Authorized King James Bible has been so widely used that until now, no one has questioned the accuracy of this translation. Some have suggested that we must accept the word 'church' simply because it has been used so long, and that it is commonly understood by most Christians. But fact remains, 'church' is not what Jesus said

He would build. Church is not the correct identity for the Body of Christ. Church was a willful mistranslation of ekklesia.

The specifics about the mistranslation is covered in greater detail in chapter four of the book, LEAVING CHURCH BECOMING EKKLESIA: *Because Jesus never said He would build a church* © 2015 by T. Lemoss Kurtz, Published by Kingdom Word Publications. The entire chapter can also be downloaded from The Ekklesia Center website. www.theekklesiacenter.org/free-resources.html

6. SHOULD I STOP USING THE WORD 'CHURCH'

Words evoke pictures. What comes to mind when you hear the words 'my church'? Do you think of the building you go to for worship? Do you think of the denomination you belong to? Both images would be wrong. Yet, these are the first two things that we usually envision when we speak of 'my church'.

To continue using the word 'church' will perpetuate the false image that has existed for so long. It will maintain the false identity that we have embraced. To continue to use the word 'church' will continue to say we are something Jesus never intended us to be.

The reality is that the word 'church' will not disappear overnight. People will still use it. It will not be avoided in the conversations you hear. Most of your Christian friends and colleagues will be using the word 'church' in their conversations with you. So, what is the solution?

You cannot change what others say. You cannot undo the many bible translations in print. You won't stop hearing 'church' in nearly every religious conversation. But, you can begin to train yourself to say something different. This will take time, and you must be intentional about what you say. Let me give you some examples.

If someone asks me, "What church do you go to?" I respond that "*I fellowship with XYZ*". Notice, I do not say that I 'go to XYZ'. That is because the idea of 'going to' is not biblical. When you and I gather with other believers it should be to fellowship. Another word I use often is 'ministry'. I often refer to "the ministry I attend" rather than "the church I go to".

If someone asks, "What time does your church service begin?" I respond with, "*We gather at* 10 a.m., or 11 a.m.", or whatever the time may be.

These three words – fellowship, gather, and ministry – can easily be substituted for the word 'church'. Most people you speak with won't be confused by what you say. They may still have the word 'church' in their mind, but you are upgrading your language to reflect your knowledge of ekklesia.

The word 'church' will not be stricken from the bibles you read. In most translations ekklesia has been mistranslated. There is nothing you can do about that. However, one thing that will help you remember the correct word, is to underline or circle the word 'church'. Use this technique to alert yourself to think about the difference in meaning. Additionally, you should write the accurate definition in the margins of your bible.

In chapter six of LEAVING CHURCH BECOMING EKKLESIA (page 104), I suggest a simple exercise that may help you. Each time you see the word 'church' in your bible, insert 'ruling council'. This will do two things:

- First, it will be a reminder to you of the authority of the ekklesia.
- Second, it will help reinforce what Jesus intended.

As a word of encouragement, when you begin making this vocabulary change, you will, inevitably, still say the word 'church' from time to time. This is a learning process. When you inadvertently say church, don't beat yourself up, this will happen. Keep working at it. I promise it will become easier.

7. SHOULD I LEAVE THE 'CHURCH' I ATTEND TO PURSUE WHAT I KNOW ABOUT EKKLESIA?

Jesus said, "You shall know the truth, and the truth shall make you free!" (John 8:32). Having the knowledge of truth does not always mean that your circumstances will immediately change. At times, the truth you have learned will conflict with the world you live in.

In the coming years, this may be a growing problem. The 'church' a person attends may have no understanding of ekklesia, or worse, they may even reject it. What should a person do who is facing this dilemma?

Although the church system is not what Jesus intended, we must also realize that strife and division are not His will either. Don't look for reasons to leave your current fellowship. If you believe the Holy Spirit is leading you to leave, consider the following guidelines:

- **Pray**. Spend time with the Lord. Seek direction for how to implement what you have learned about ekklesia.

- **Know the facts.** Learn the facts about ekklesia. More and more resources are becoming available. Research this subject with other believers. Don't follow hearsay! Know the facts.

- **Be open with your intentions to leave**. Don't take any actions in secret. If you are serving under 'church leadership' respect it. Get their views on ekklesia, and share with them what you have learned. Many times, you can learn from those who don't understand or disagree with your stance.

- **Don't criticize the church you are leaving**. New revelation is not a license to demean those who don't have it yet.

Most likely, you learned the truth about ekklesia AFTER someone else. How would you feel if they had humiliated you because you didn't know what they did? Spend time sharing what you know. Invite them to study with you. Encourage them to seek answers on their own.

- **Respect the church system you leave**. Leaving a ministry can be difficult. However, don't speak negatively against the ministry you leave, even if you believe that you were treated unfairly when you left. Negative conversations can give the impression that you are not sure of your actions and you are trying to justify yourself. If you believe the Lord is leading you to leave, limit your conversation to your decision alone.

- **Don't invite others to follow you.** If the Lord leads you to leave a ministry, do not invite others to follow you. Allow others to hear from the Lord for themselves.

WARNING: This is not to advocate leaving churches. But, if the decision is made to do so, we strongly encourage people to do it with honesty and integrity.

8. ARE THERE LEADERS IN THE EKKLESIA?

Yes. Scripture reveals three categories of earthly leadership in the ekklesia. They are governmental leaders, developmental leaders and service leaders.

The governmental leaders are the elders that oversee local, city and regional ekklesia. The elders provide a safe atmosphere for the believers to function. Elders are usually appointed by apostles, who are also elders (Acts 14:23; Titus 1:5; 1Peter 5:1).

The developmental leaders are the five-fold ministers of apostles, prophets, evangelists, pastors and teachers. Their purpose is to equip, perfect or bring the saints to maturity to do the work of ministry (Ephesians 4:11-12).

The third category are the deacons. They appear to serve in close proximity to the elders. The Greek word *diakonos*, from which the word deacon is translated, suggests that this ministry provides service to and for the Body of Christ.

There is a clear difference in leadership found in the 'church system' and that in the ekklesia. In the church, leadership is hierarchal. It is from the top down. In the ekklesia, leadership serves from the bottom. They support the saints as they do the work of ministry.

Elders, protect them from wolves who would prey on the weaker saints. They help protect them from false doctrine. The spiritual feed those entrusted to them (Acts 20:28-30; 1Peter 5:1). Five-fold ministers serve to bring the saints to maturity. Showing them how to be a body fitly joined together (Ephesians 4:16). And although no specific tasks are mentioned in scripture, the deacons most likely served to help provide the flow of resources among the Body of Christ.

Yes, the ekklesia has leadership. They are not hierarchal, but rather divine functions that strengthen the saints as they expand the Kingdom of God in the earth.

EXERCISES

EXERCISE A: WHAT ARE WE DOING?

AS BELIEVERS, WE MUST UNDERSTAND THAT WE ARE CALLED OUT TO REPRESENT JESUS, AND HIS GOVERNMENT – THE KINGDOM OF HEAVEN.

Make a list of three or more things that your gathering is doing to represent the Kingdom of Heaven?

WHAT ARE YOU DOING? THE FACT THAT JESUS IS LORD IN YOUR LIFE MUST BE EVIDENT AT ALL TIMES. LIST 3 THINGS YOU WILL DO TO EXPRESS THAT JESUS IS LORD IN YOUR LIFE?

EXERCISE B: DECLARING THE LORDSHIP OF JESUS CHRIST

KEY: Entrance into the ekklesia is given to those who have the revelation that Jesus is the Christ, Son of the Living God. It is important that you declare His Lordship over every aspect of your life.

Read the following passages and discuss the questions below.

Romans 10:9-10 That if thou shalt confess with thy mouth the Lord Jesus, and shalt believe in thine heart that God hath raised him from the dead, thou shalt be saved. 10 For with the heart man believeth unto righteousness; and with the mouth confession is made unto salvation.

How often should you confess that Jesus is Lord?

HINT: Matthew 16:16; John 6:69; John 11:27; Acts 2:36

Matthew 16:17 And Jesus answered and said unto him, Blessed art thou, Simon Barjona: for flesh and blood hath not revealed it unto thee, but my Father which is in heaven.

How is the Lordship of Jesus Christ revealed to us?

HINT: John 15:26; 1Corinthians 2:9-10; 1Corinthians12:3;

Why is it important to confess the Lordship of Jesus Christ with your mouth?

```
_____
_____
_____
_____
_____
```

Why is it important to believe that Jesus is Lord in your heart?

```
_____
_____
_____
_____
```

Can you do one without the other? Why or why not?

```
_____
_____
_____
_____
```

EXERCISE C: The ekklesia has a clear assignment and purpose in the earth. The following passages gives a view of ekklesia. Read and discuss each of the following.

> **Suggested Reading:** LEAVING CHURCH BECOMING EKKLESIA, Chapter 8, Ekklesia Today, Page 129

Matthew 16:18-19 And I say also unto thee, That thou art Peter, and upon this rock I will build my church; and the gates of hell shall not prevail against it. 19 And I will give unto thee the keys of the kingdom of heaven: and whatsoever thou shalt bind on earth shall be bound in heaven: and whatsoever thou shalt loose on earth shall be loosed in heaven.

> a **REVIEW PAGE 27:** How will you know you have the keys of the Kingdom of Heaven?
>
> b Discuss the importance of binding and loosing in the 21st century. See Page 137 LEAVING CHURCH BECOMING EKKLESIA

<table>
<tr><td></td></tr>
<tr><td></td></tr>
<tr><td></td></tr>
<tr><td></td></tr>
<tr><td></td></tr>
</table>

Ephesians 3:10 To the intent that now unto the principalities and powers in heavenly places might be known by the [ekklesia] the manifold wisdom of God,

a Discuss strategies for demonstrating Gods wisdom. Create a list of these strategies

1Timothy 3:15 But if I tarry long, that thou mayest know how thou oughtest to behave thyself in the house of God, which is the [ekklesia] of the living God, the pillar and ground of the truth.

How does the revelation of Jesus Christ in my life effect my faith?

What is the difference between believing IN God, and BELIEVING GOD?

EXERCISE D: It is important that you understand the difference between 'church' and 'ekklesia'. In this exercise do your own research of the word 'church'.

Review Page 17: Ekklesia Explained

Suggested Reading: LEAVING CHURCH BECOMING EKKLESIA, Chapter 4, How Ekklesia Became Church, Page 49

17 QUICK FACTS

1. **Ekklesia** is a Greek word found 115 times in the original language of the bible. The New Testament was originally written in Greek.

2. **Ekklesia** generally refers to a group of people who are 'called out'.

3. **Ekklesia** could be translated into English as 'assembly' or 'congregation' but not as 'church'.

4. **Ekklesia** was understood by the people in Jesus' day to be a group of people called out to conduct the affairs of the government. Therefore, ekklesia could also be called 'ruling council'.

5. **Ekklesia** is NOT the Greek word for Church. The word 'CHURCH' is a mistranslation of the Greek word 'ekklesia'.

6. **Ekklesia** was mistranslated on purpose by the instructions of King James in 1611.

7. Only Jesus can build His ekklesia (*Matthew 16:18*).

8. Jesus purchased the ekklesia with His blood (Acts 20:28).

9. The ekklesia has the authority to bind and loose on earth whatever has been bound and loosed in heaven (*Matthew 16:19*).

10. The Gates of Hades cannot prevail over the ekklesia (*Matthew 16:19*).

11. The ekklesia has the Keys of the Kingdom of Heaven (*Matthew 16:19*).

12. The ekklesia is the pillar and ground of truth (1Timothy 3:15).

13. The wisdom of God is made known to principalities and powers in heavenly places by the ekklesia (*Ephesians 3:10*).

14. You are a member of the Lord's ekklesia and walk in the power of the Lord (Mark 16:17).

15. The ekklesia is the Body of Christ (*Ephesians 1:22*).

16. Jesus is the Head of the ekklesia (*Ephesians 1:23*).

17. Apostles and prophets are the foundation of the ekklesia (Ephesians 2:20).

To learn more, visit our website

www.TheEkklesiaCenter.org

Made in the USA
Coppell, TX
16 March 2024

30162786R00036